J B Lee
Vande
Confe
Gene

W9-BGS-062

$26.65
ocn244354521
10/08/2009

WE THE PEOPLE

CONFEDERATE COMMANDER
GENERAL ROBERT E. LEE

by Sue Vander Hook

Content Adviser: Lisa Laskin, Ph.D.,
Lecturer on History, Harvard University

Reading Adviser: Alexa L. Sandmann, Ed.D.,
Professor of Literacy, College and Graduate School
of Education, Health, and Human Services,
Kent State University

Compass Point Books ◆ Minneapolis, Minnesota

Compass Point Books
151 Good Counsel Drive
P.O. Box 669
Mankato, MN 56002-0669

This book was manufactured with paper containing at least 10 percent post-consumer waste.

On the cover: Robert E. Lee and his generals

Photographs ©: The Granger Collection, New York, cover, 15, 17, 25, 27, 28, 31, 32; Corbis/Royalty-Free,
4, 26, 36; Library of Congress, 5, 6; Classic Image/Alamy, 9; M. Timothy O'Keefe/Alamy, 10; North
Wind Picture Archives, 13, 35, 38; Courtesy National Park Service, Arlington House, 18 (all); Hulton
Archive/Getty Images, 20; Private Collection/Look and Learn/The Bridgeman Art Library, 22, 37; Zack
Frank/Shutterstock, 40.

Editor: Robert McConnell
Page Production: Heidi Thompson
Photo Researcher: Svetlana Zhurkin
Cartographer: XNR Productions, Inc.
Library Consultant: Kathleen Baxter

Art Director: LuAnn Ascheman-Adams
Creative Director: Joe Ewest
Editorial Director: Nick Healy
Managing Editor: Catherine Neitge

Library of Congress Cataloging-in-Publication Data
Vander Hook, Sue.
  Confederate commander : General Robert E. Lee / by Sue Vander Hook.
    p. cm.—(We the people)
  Includes index.
  ISBN 978-0-7565-4107-1 (library. binding.)
  1. Lee, Robert E. (Robert Edward), 1807–1870—Juvenile literature. 2. Lee, Robert E. (Robert Edward),
1807–1870—Military leadership—Juvenile literature. 3. Generals—Confederate States of America—
Biography—Juvenile literature. 4. Confederate States of America. Army—Biography—Juvenile literature.
5. United States—History—Civil War, 1861–1865—Campaigns—Juvenile literature. I. Title. II. Title:
General Robert E. Lee.
  E467.1.L4E54 2009
  973.7'3092—dc22
  [B]   2008035718

Visit Compass Point Books on the Internet at *www.compasspointbooks.com*
or e-mail your request to *custserv@compasspointbooks.com*

Table of Contents

1

Loyal to the South

$\mathcal{R}$obert E. Lee finally stopped pacing and sat down in a chair. Exhausted from worry and lack of sleep, he picked up a pen and began writing to General Winfield Scott, his superior officer and longtime friend: "General … I have felt that I ought not longer to retain my commission in the Army. I therefore tender my resignation." Lee was giving up a 36-year career in the U.S. Army. He was also turning his back on the United States of America, the country he loved. But he could

The outbreak of war forced Robert E. Lee to choose between two loyalties.

not serve a country that might attack his fellow Southerners and perhaps his own state. "How can I draw my sword upon Virginia, my native state?" he had asked Scott.

It was April 20, 1861. Just eight days before, Southern soldiers had fired on Fort Sumter in Charleston, South Carolina. That event marked the beginning of what would be called the American Civil War.

Fort Sumter, defended by fewer than 100 Union soldiers,
was captured by more than 5,000 Confederate troops.

South Carolina had seceded from the Union in December 1860. It no longer wanted to be part of the United States. Six other Southern states soon followed. On February 4, 1861, these seven states formed their own country—the Confederate States of America. Lee's home state of Virginia was the next to secede. Eventually 11 Southern states formed the Confederacy.

After the attack on Fort Sumter, the newly elected president of the United States, Abraham Lincoln, took action. He asked for 75,000 volunteers to fight in South Carolina. Lincoln wanted Lee to lead the Union Army. If Lee accepted, he would become

General Winfield Scott wrote that Lee was "the very best soldier I ever saw in the field."

a general, the highest-ranking officer. But Lee turned down the president's offer. He couldn't turn his back on Virginia or his Southern neighbors. General Scott told him, "Lee, you have made the greatest mistake of your life."

For the next four years, the Civil War raged. North and South clashed in bloody battles that pitted Americans against Americans and brother against brother. The biggest issue was slavery. Lincoln, like many people in the North, opposed allowing slavery in new Western states. Other people, in both the North and the South, thought each new state should decide for itself. Then there were those who wanted slavery preserved at all costs. Most people in the Confederacy believed it was necessary for the Southern economy.

Lee's decision to remain faithful to the South cost him dearly. He lost his U.S. citizenship and sealed his destiny with that of the Confederacy.

2 Boy From Virginia

Robert Edward Lee was born on January 19, 1807, in Westmoreland County, Virginia. He was the fifth child of Henry Lee III and Ann Carter Lee. Two more children would eventually complete the Lee family.

Robert's father had quite a reputation as a Revolutionary War hero. His nickname was "Light-Horse Harry," for his swift surprise raids against the British. Robert's mother was from a large, wealthy family. For generations, they had owned vast lands and many slaves. But Robert didn't get to enjoy their fame and wealth for long. When he was only 1 year old, his father lost most of his money because of failed land ventures. Writing bad checks then landed Light-Horse Harry in prison.

Robert was 3 when his father got out of prison. Henry Lee's troubles still weren't over. Two years later, he was injured in a

After the Revolutionary War, Henry Lee III served as governor of Virginia and a member of Congress.

riot in Baltimore. When he tried to protect a friend from an angry

mob, he was beaten up and left with lifelong injuries and pain.

The next year, Henry Lee left his family and sailed to the West

Indies. Robert never saw his father again. Henry tried to return to

Virginia when Robert was 11, but he died on the voyage home.

Robert attended a family boys' school, at the home of an

Robert E. Lee was born at Stratford Hall plantation, which was between Richmond, Virginia, and Washington, D.C.

aunt, for six years. At age 13, he attended Alexandria Academy. Robert did well in school, especially in algebra and geometry. He was a quiet teenager who took his responsibilities seriously. At home he helped his mother manage the bills and the servants. He was close to his mother, who raised six children alone (one had died in infancy) and taught them important values. She taught Robert that complaining was rude and showed a failure to trust God. Robert took her religious teachings to heart. He often wrote in his letters about events that were "God's will."

At 17, Robert applied to the U.S. Military Academy at West Point, New York. A year later, he was accepted. There he could receive an education at no cost to his family and become an officer in the Army.

3

West Point

The rules at West Point were strict. Those who broke them got demerits, which were marks against them. Cadets, as academy students are called, got demerits for fighting, drinking alcohol, playing cards, or being late. They couldn't have visitors, leave the academy grounds without permission, or read books or magazines except when doing course assignments. Robert E. Lee was the first West Point cadet to receive no demerits. His perfect behavior earned him the nickname "Marble Man" because he was strong and didn't crack under pressure.

Cadets were trained to fight, but they also learned to be engineers. When they graduated as officers, they would join the Army Corps of Engineers and be able to build roads, bridges, forts, and dams to help the growing nation.

In 1829, at the age of 22, Lee graduated with high honors.

The U.S. Military Academy was established in 1802, only 23 years before Robert E. Lee became a cadet.

He had the second-highest grades in his class of 46 cadets. Lee was now a second lieutenant in the Army Corps of Engineers. But before he went to work for the Army, he went home. He was eager to see his mother. However, Ann Carter Lee was very sick, and on July 26, 1829, she died. The rest of the summer, Lee mourned her death.

4 Army, Marriage, and Children

*I*n August 1829, Robert E. Lee began his first job with the Army Corps of Engineers. It was not a pleasant assignment. He worked on Cockspur Island near Savannah, Georgia. The heat and mosquitoes were awful. He built ditches and dikes, which are used to control water. Heavy storms often ruined them.

The following year, Lee took a vacation in Virginia. He spent time with Mary Custis, a longtime friend of the family. The Custis family was famous. Mary's father was George Washington Parke Custis, a stepgrandson of former President George Washington. He owned several large plantations, including a large farm called Arlington near Washington, D.C.

Lee asked Mary Custis to marry him, and they were married on June 30, 1831. Their first home was simple Army quarters at Fort Monroe in Virginia. But they were happy. In a letter to a friend, Lee wrote, "I would not be unmarried for all you could offer me."

Their first child arrived on September 16, 1832. They named him George Washington Custis Lee, after Mary's father. He was called Master Custis. Lee said he was the most darling boy in the world.

In 1834, the Army made Lee the assistant to the chief of engineers in Washington. However, the Lees couldn't find a suitable place to live there. So they stayed at Arlington with Mary's parents.

Mary Custis Lee was a great-granddaughter of first lady Martha Washington.

Every day, Lee traveled to work on horseback, a half-hour ride each way. The Lees didn't know that Arlington would be their home for 30 years.

The Army sent Lee all over the country. While Mary and Custis stayed at Arlington, Lee traveled for months at a time. In 1835, he helped set the boundary line between Ohio and Michigan. Two years later he worked on the harbor at St. Louis, Missouri. His men made it easier for boats to travel on the Mississippi and Missouri rivers.

Lee missed his family, which had grown by now. He wrote to a friend, "I am the father of three children ... so entwined around my heart that I feel them at every pulsation [heartbeat]." He wrote many letters to his wife, who was expecting their fourth child. Lee wrote in one letter, "You do not know how much I have missed you and the children, my dear Mary."

In October 1840, Lee returned to Arlington, to his wife and

four children—Custis, 8; Mary, 6; William (called Rooney), 4; and Annie, 1. Early in 1841, he was home for the birth of their fifth child, Eleanor, whom they called Agnes.

St. Louis was an important port of call for steamboats carrying passengers and freight.

George Washington Custis Lee

Mary Custis Lee

William Henry Fitzhugh "Rooney" Lee

Anne Carter Lee

Eleanor Agnes Lee

Robert Edward Lee Jr.

Mildred Childe Lee

Lee's Army duties often kept him away from his home, his wife, Mary, and their children.

The Army now had a job for Lee in Brooklyn, New York.

He would be supervising the repair of four old forts. This

time Mary and the children came with him. They lived at Fort

Hamilton, in Brooklyn, although Mary and the children spent

winters at Arlington. In 1843, Mary gave birth to a son, Robert

Edward Lee Jr. The couple's seventh and last child, Mildred, was

born in 1846.

Lee was now a captain in the Army. But he longed to be on

the battlefield. He wanted to be a soldier, not an engineer who

dug ditches and fixed buildings. He was about to get his wish.

5

At War With Mexico

*I*n 1846, Robert E. Lee went to Texas, where he served under General Winfield Scott. Texas had become a state in December 1845, but Mexico and the United States could not agree on the new border. Then U.S. General Zachary Taylor built a fort on the disputed border— the Rio Grande. The Mexican army attacked. In May 1846, the United States declared war on Mexico.

Lee had gone to Texas to survey land in the new state. Now he found him-

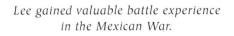

Lee gained valuable battle experience in the Mexican War.

self in the middle of a war. With his knowledge of the terrain, he helped soldiers find their way around Texas. He made accurate maps that helped soldiers carry out surprise attacks. His days often began at 3 A.M. and ended after he had traveled 60 miles (96 kilometers) on horseback. His keen eye for detail and his engineering abilities were important to the soldiers. General Scott greatly valued Lee's advice.

Lee often put his skills to work in the war. He was promoted many times, finally receiving the rank of colonel. His brilliance and courage led General Scott to write that Lee was "the very best soldier I ever saw in the field."

The war officially ended on February 2, 1848. Under a treaty the United States paid Mexico $15 million for land that stretched from Texas to California. The U.S. government also declared the Rio Grande to be the official border. Problems involving Texas weren't over, however. Americans disagreed

Lee's actions had played an important role in the capture of the Mexican fortress at Chapultepec by General Scott's troops on their way to Mexico City.

about whether slavery should be legal in Texas and other new states. The country was divided. The slavery issue would also divide Lee's loyalties and change his life.

6 Prelude to War

The Army next sent Robert E. Lee to Baltimore, Maryland, a city near Washington. He looked forward to an interesting assignment, but he was told to repair another fort. Mary and the children also came to Baltimore, which made it more enjoyable.

In 1850, Lee's oldest son, 18-year-old Custis Lee, followed in his father's footsteps. He enrolled in the Military Academy at West Point. Two years later the Army appointed his father superintendent of the academy. Robert E. Lee returned to his alma mater and joined his son. The Lee family lived on the grounds.

Lee was there three years. Then, in 1856, after joining the cavalry, he went back to Texas to command a group of soldiers who protected American settlers from attacks by Native Americans. The death of Mary's father in 1857 brought Lee back to Virginia. They had inherited Arlington, the large Custis plantation. Lee took time off from the Army to manage his father-in-law's house and land.

While Lee was in Virginia, the slavery issue was heating up. In October 1859, about 20 men, led by abolitionist John Brown, took over the federal arsenal at Harpers Ferry, in what is now West Virginia. President James Buchanan ordered Lee to capture the men.

When Lee and his soldiers arrived at Harpers Ferry, the abolitionists, who wanted slavery to be banned, had taken hostages and locked themselves in a firehouse. "Surrender or be attacked," Lee warned them. The message was unheeded. Lee's soldiers attacked. Some abolitionists were wounded or killed, and John Brown was caught and later hanged.

Lee returned to Texas. In November 1860, Abraham Lincoln was elected president on the Republican Party's anti-slavery platform. Many Southerners were enraged that the anti-

It took Lee's men less than an hour to defeat the abolitionists at Harpers Ferry.

slavery candidate had won. In the next three months seven

Southern states seceded from the United States. They formed

their own country—the Confederate States of America. Jefferson

Davis, of Mississippi, became their president. When the seventh

state, Texas, left the Union, the Army, including Lee, was ordered

to leave the state.

Lee went home to Virginia, where state leaders were talking about secession. Lee's loyalties were divided. He didn't think the country should split. He also didn't want the national government telling the states what to do.

On April 12, 1861, Confederate soldiers fired on the U.S. Army's Fort Sumter in South Carolina. The Civil War had begun. A few days later Lee was summoned to Washington. President Lincoln wanted him to lead a large army to stop the Southern rebellion. But Lee could not accept Lincoln's offer. He would not

Jefferson Davis was president of the Confederate States of America throughout the Civil War.

attack Southern states. In a letter to General Winfield Scott, Lee resigned from the Army.

Virginia seceded from the Union on April 17. Lee accepted Jefferson Davis' offer to join the Confederate cause. He became the commander of Virginia's military forces. Finally he had an exciting assignment, but he was leading a small, poorly equipped army. He also was fighting against the country he had long served.

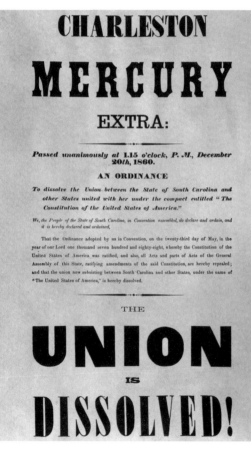

A newspaper's poster, called a broadside, announced South Carolina's decision to separate from the United States.

7   The Civil War

By June 1861 three more Southern states had seceded. The total number of Confederate states was now 11. In July the

Confederate volunteers posed for a Richmond photographer before the First Battle of Bull Run.

first Civil War battle, the First Battle of Bull Run, was fought at Manassas, Virginia. The Confederate Army won.

President Davis then sent Robert E. Lee to western Virginia. Lee's soldiers made sure Union troops didn't reach Richmond, the Confederate capital. Davis then promoted Lee to general and assigned him to the coast of South Carolina. There soldiers built ditches and dirt walls for protection in battle. Lee's engineering experience was coming in handy. His men, apparently thinking he would rather dig than fight, nicknamed him the "King of Spades."

Lee led Confederate troops in some of the Civil War's most important battles.

Lee went to Richmond for a while to advise President Davis. In May 1862, he returned to the battlefield. Lee soon renamed his forces the Army of Northern Virginia. Union forces under General George McClellan were within 7 miles (11 km) of Richmond, dangerously close.

Lee's soldiers tried to hold them back. Over seven days, from June 25 to July 1, 1862, six major battles were fought. They came to be called the Seven Days Battles. Lee's forces drove McClellan's troops from the Richmond area, and he was hailed as a military genius.

Lee's strategy was to always stay on the offensive—one step ahead of the Union Army. General Thomas "Stonewall" Jackson and General J.E.B. "Jeb" Stuart helped him carry out this plan. Stuart led the cavalry, which spent hours every day on horseback searching for Northern troops.

In August the Confederates were again victorious under

In a daring scouting maneuver before the Seven Days Battles, Confederate General J.E.B. "Jeb" Stuart led his cavalrymen completely around the Union forces.

Lee's leadership. They won the Second Battle of Bull Run

at Manassas. But in September, after one day of fighting at

Sharpsburg, Maryland, 10,000 Confederate soldiers were dead, wounded, or missing. After the Battle of Antietam, as it was called, Lee's forces were pushed back to Virginia.

The Confederate Army was in bad shape. After a year of fighting, soldiers were barely surviving. Lee wrote to President Davis, "The army ... lacks much of the material of war, is feeble in transportation, the animals

Thomas J. "Stonewall" Jackson was one of Lee's most effective generals.

being much reduced, and the men are poorly provided with clothes, and in thousands of instances are destitute of [lack] shoes."

Lee was also burdened by troubles at home. Union soldiers had captured Arlington, forcing his wife, Mary, to leave. She now lived in a rented house in Richmond. Mary was suffering from severe arthritis, and daughter Agnes was taking care of her. Custis was serving on Jefferson Davis' staff. Rooney and young Robert were fighting in the Confederate Army. Daughter Mary was living with friends, and 16-year-old Mildred was at boarding school. Tragedy struck hardest in October 1862, when 23-year-old daughter Annie died of typhoid fever.

It would be two and a half years before one of Lee's burdens—the burden of war—would be lifted.

8 The Tide Turns

$\mathcal{R}$obert E. Lee continued to win battles, for a while. The Confederates defeated the Union at the Battle of Fredericksburg in November 1862. Victory also belonged to the South at the Battle of Chancellorsville in spring 1863. General Stonewall Jackson was badly wounded in that battle, however, and he died eight days later. It was a great loss for Lee and his troops.

The Battle of Gettysburg in southern Pennsylvania in July 1863 was a dramatic and costly defeat for the South. The Confederates were mowed down by Union cannon fire. After the battle, 28,000 of the 75,000 Southern soldiers were dead, wounded, or missing. Union casualties were 23,000 of 83,000 men. What was left of Lee's ragtag army retreated to Virginia.

For a while, Lee's popularity faded. The newspapers blamed him for losing at Gettysburg. Some said Lee blamed himself. He offered to resign. In a letter to Jefferson Davis,

Lee wrote that it would be the happiest day of his life if the

Confederate Army's commander were "a worthy leader—one that

would accomplish more than I could perform and all that I have

wished." Davis replied, "Our country could not bear to lose you."

Lee visited Mary at Richmond that December, and again

Confederate soldiers charged up Little Round Top hill
during the Battle of Gettysburg.

General Ulysses S. Grant was known for his aggressiveness and determination.

there were family troubles. Mary's arthritis had forced her to use a wheelchair. Rooney had been captured by the Union Army. Rooney's wife died in late December. Furthermore, the U.S. government was planning to use Arlington for its military headquarters.

In March 1864, President Lincoln put General Ulysses S. Grant in charge of the Union Army. Grant's master plan to attack the South sealed Lee's fate. Lee showed brilliance on the battlefield and inflicted heavy casualties on the enemy. But the Confederates were defeated in battle after battle, and their numbers shrank. Finally they were pushed out of Richmond itself.

Grant asked Lee to surrender. With his troops exhausted and starving, Lee had no choice. Lee and Grant met on April 9, 1865, at Appomattox Court House, Virginia. Grant wrote the terms of surrender, and Lee signed the document. Grant respected Lee, and he gave food to Lee's starving troops. He also let them keep their horses and go home.

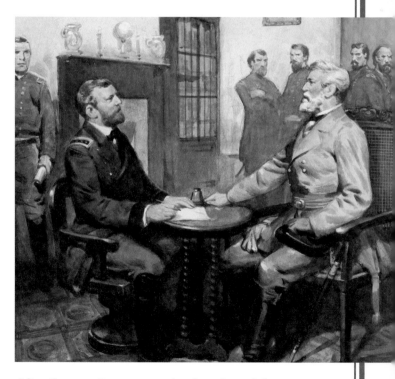

After the war, Grant wrote that he admired the courage of the Confederates and felt sympathy for their defeat.

Lee said to his soldiers, "Men, we have fought through the war together. I have done my best for you; my heart is too full to say more." The soldiers put down their weapons and rode to

Lee fondly said goodbye to his men after the surrender at Appomattox.

Richmond. The crowds there welcomed Lee as a hero.

Jefferson Davis was arrested and held in prison for two years. But Lee was not punished. Grant said Lee had promised never to fight again, and he persuaded President Andrew Johnson not to put him on trial.

What would Lee do now? He thought about farming, but in August 1865, Washington College in Lexington, Virginia, asked him to become its president. Lee accepted. He enjoyed his work at the college and helped it grow.

Lee was not through serving the nation, however. He encouraged Southerners to put the Civil War behind them and move forward in unity. This was important at a time when many people in the South were angry about losing the war and bitter toward their former enemy.

Lee's health grew worse. In the spring and summer of 1870, he took a break from work and traveled in the South. He returned to work in the fall, but by late September he was bedridden.

On October 12, 1870, Robert E. Lee died, at the age

of 63. He was buried in Lexington, Virginia, in the chapel

A statue of Robert E. Lee astride his horse, Traveller, tops a monument to Virginians at Gettysburg National Military Park. A similar statue is in Richmond, Virginia.

at Washington College (today called Washington and Lee University). Lee's horse, Traveller, walked behind the hearse that carried Lee's body. When Traveller died the following year, he was buried near the chapel entrance.

To some, Lee was a man who was deeply committed to his beliefs. To others, he was a slave owner who wrongly fought to defend slavery. Ultimately Robert E. Lee will be remembered as a great general and an important figure in the history of the United States.

Glossary

abolitionist—person who supported the banning of slavery

arsenal—storehouse of weapons and ammunition

Confederate States of America—Southern states that seceded from the Union and fought against the Northern states in the Civil War; also called the Confederacy

plantation—large farm in the South, usually worked by slaves

platform—statement of political goals made by members of a political party

quarters—housing used by the military

ragtag—ragged and tattered

rebellion—fight against a government or ruler

secede—withdraw from

Union—Northern states that fought against the Southern states in the Civil War

ventures—business activities

Did You Know?

- Robert E. Lee's grandfather, Richard Henry Lee, was a lawmaker who urged the colonies to become independent from Great Britain and signed the Declaration of Independence.

- Lee's father once wrote a bad check to George Washington.

- The Carter family (Lee's mother's family) was so large that they had their own schools—one for boys, which Lee attended, and one for girls.

- Lee was well-liked at West Point; a classmate later wrote, "No other youth … so united the qualities that win warm friendship and command high respect."

- Lee's wife, Mary, was raised as an only child after all her brothers and sisters had died as infants; she was used to a lot of attention and having servants who did everything for her.

- During a battle in the Mexican War, Lee stayed awake for 36 hours straight, riding through dangerous territory to find a way for U.S. soldiers to make a surprise raid on the Mexican army.

- Lee's soldiers sometimes were so hungry that they took food from farmers; some farmers were given a receipt that they could use to be paid in Confederate dollars, but Confederate money soon became worthless.

Important Dates

Timeline

1807	Born January 19 in Westmoreland County, Virginia
1829	Graduates from the U.S. Military Academy; his mother, Ann Carter Lee, dies July 26
1831	Marries Mary Custis; they eventually have seven children
1846	Serves in the Mexican War
1852	Appointed superintendent of the U.S. Military Academy
1859	Attacks abolitionists at Harpers Ferry
1861	The Civil War begins; the Confederate States of America is formed; Lee resigns from the U.S. Army and assumes command of the Army of Northern Virginia
1863	The Confederates lose the Battle of Gettysburg
1865	Surrenders to General Ulysses S. Grant April 9; the Civil War ends
1870	Dies October 12 and is buried at Washington College (now Washington and Lee University)

Important People

Jefferson Davis (1808–1889)
President of the Confederate States of America during the Civil War; although charged with treason, he was released from prison after two years and never tried; he died December 6, 1889

General Ulysses S. Grant (1822–1885)
Commander of the Union Army at the end of the Civil War; he was elected president of the United States and served from 1869 to 1877; he died of throat cancer July 23, 1885

General Thomas "Stonewall" Jackson (1824–1863)
Confederate general who fought with Lee during the Civil War; he was shot accidentally by his own troops at the Battle of Chancellorsville in 1863 and died eight days later

Abraham Lincoln (1809–1865)
President of the United States from 1861 to 1865; he led the nation through the Civil War and in 1863 issued the Emancipation Proclamation, which freed slaves in the Confederacy; he was assassinated April 14, 1865

General Winfield Scott (1786–1866)
U.S. Army general, nicknamed "Old Rough and Ready," who commanded troops in the War of 1812 and the Mexican War, and at the beginning of the Civil War; he died May 29, 1866

Want to Know More?

More Books to Read

Burgan, Michael. *Fort Sumter*. Minneapolis: Compass Point Books, 2006.

McPherson, James M. *Fields of Fury: The American Civil War*. New York: Atheneum Books for Young Readers, 2002.

Ransom, Candice F. *Robert E. Lee*. Minneapolis: Lerner Publications, 2005.

Robertson, James I. Jr. *Robert E. Lee: Virginian Soldier, American Citizen*. New York: Atheneum Books for Young Readers, 2005.

Santella, Andrew. *Surrender at Appomattox*. Minneapolis: Compass Point Books, 2006.

On the Web

For more information on this topic, use FactHound.

1. Go to *www.facthound.com*

2. Choose your grade level.

3. Begin your search.

This book's ID number is 9780756541071

FactHound will find the best sites for you.

On the Road

Arlington House, the Robert E. Lee Memorial
George Washington Memorial Parkway
Turkey Run Park
McLean, VA 22101
703/235-1530
Home of Robert E. Lee has a museum and offers tours of the house and flower garden

Lee Chapel and Museum
Washington and Lee University
Lexington, VA 24450
540/458-8768
Features a tour of Robert E. Lee's university office and Civil War exhibits in the chapel he designed; location of the Lee family crypt

Look for more We the People Biographies:

American Patriot: Benjamin Franklin
Civil War Spy: Elizabeth Van Lew
Confederate General: Stonewall Jackson
First of First Ladies: Martha Washington
A Signer for Independence: John Hancock
Soldier and Founder: Alexander Hamilton
Union General and 18th President: Ulysses S. Grant

A complete list of We the People titles is available on our Web site:
www.compasspointbooks.com

Index

About the Author

Sue Vander Hook has been writing and editing books for nearly 20 years. Although her writing career began with several nonfiction books for adults, her main focus is educational books for children and young adults. She especially enjoys writing about historical events and biographies of people who made a difference. Her published works also include a high school curriculum and several series on disease, technology, and sports. Sue lives with her family in Minnesota.